		DATE DUE	

International Organizations

The Red Cross

Krista McLuskey

WEIGL PUBLISHERS INC.

Dedication

This series is dedicated to those people who help make their community, state, and world a better place. Volunteering is one way to become an active and responsible citizen. The thoughtfulness and hard work of volunteers is an inspiration to all. International Organizations is both an acknowledgment of and a tribute to volunteers.

Credits

Project Coordinator
Michael Lowry
Copy Editor
Heather Kissock
Photo Researcher
Gayle Murdoff
Design and Layout
Warren Clark
Bryan Pezzi

Published by Weigl Publishers Inc.
123 South Broad Street, Box 227
Mankato, MN 56002
USA

Web site: www.weigl.com
Copyright ©2003 WEIGL PUBLISHERS INC.

Library of Congress Cataloging-in-Publication Data

McLuskey, Krista, 1974-
  Red Cross / Krista McLuskey.
      p. cm. -- (International organizations)
Summary: Provides a history of the Red Cross, including its members, mission, goals, and achievements, plus case studies of individuals who have benefited from the work of this international service organization.

Includes bibliographical references and index.
  ISBN 1-59036-019-2 (library binding : alk. paper)
  1. Red Cross--Juvenile literature. [1. Red Cross.] I. Title. II. Series.
  HV568 .M34 2002
  361.7'7--dc21
                                                            2002006561

Printed in Canada
1 2 3 4 5 6 7 8 9 0   06 05 04 03 02

Photo Credits

Every reasonable effort has been made to trace ownership and to obtain permission to reprint copyright material. The publishers would be pleased to have any errors or omissions brought to their attention so that they may be corrected in subsequent printings.

Cover: American Red Cross; **American Red Cross:** pages 7, 19, 20, 27; **Neil Cooper:** pages 15, 25; **Corbis Corporation:** page 13; **Corel Corporation:** page 14; **Howard Davies/Exile Images:** pages 3, 5, 9, 10, 12, 23 top, 23 bottom, 26; **Greg Martin/ Corbis Sygma/MAGMA:** page 18; **National Archives of Canada:** pages 21 (PA1781), 22 (PA-116510).

Contents

What is the Red Cross?

With more than 115 million volunteers, the Red Cross is the largest volunteer organization in the world. The official name of the Red Cross is the "International Red Cross and Red Crescent Movement." For more than a century, Red Cross workers have provided **humanitarian** aid and assistance to those in need. In times of war, workers help ease the suffering of soldiers, civilians, and prisoners. The Red Cross also works in times of peace to assist victims of natural disasters, such as famines, disease, floods, and hurricanes.

The International Red Cross and Red Crescent Movement consists of 178 national Red Cross and Red Crescent societies from around the world. The national societies, such as the American Red Cross, are connected by the International Committee of the Red Cross (ICRC) and the International Federation of Red Cross and Red Crescent Societies.

With its headquarters in Geneva, Switzerland, the ICRC organizes the national societies during times of conflict to help victims of war and violence. The ICRC also works to promote international humanitarian law.

The International Federation of Red Cross and Red Crescent Societies coordinates relief operations during natural disasters. The federation is also based in Geneva.

> **"For the Red Cross there is no just war and no unjust war—there are only victims in need of help."**
> **Jean Pictet, ICRC**

Quick Fact ·

The Red Cross emblem was adopted at the first Geneva Convention in 1864. The emblem, a red cross on a white background, was a reversal of the colors of the Swiss flag.

During times of armed conflict, the neutrality of the Red Cross ensures that it is able to provide relief assistance to those who need it most.

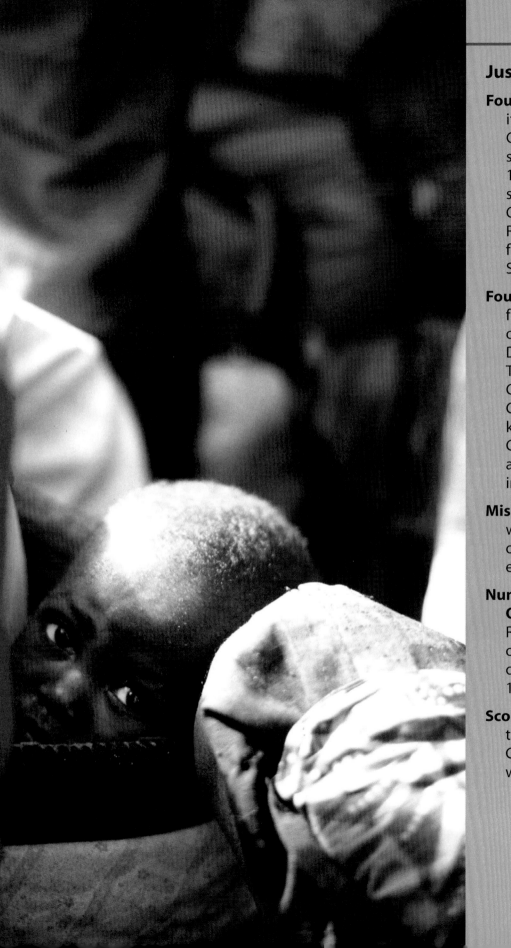

Just the Facts

Founded: The ICRC held its first conference in Geneva in 1863. A second conference, in 1864, resulted in the signing of the Geneva Convention. A national Red Cross society was formed in the United States in 1881.

Founders: Henry Dunant first developed the idea of the Red Cross. Henry Dunant, Louis Appia, Theodore Maunoir, Gustave Moynier, and G. H. Dufour became known as the Committee of Five, and turned the idea into reality.

Mission: To help those who suffer in times of war and other emergencies.

Number of Member Organizations: The Red Cross consists of two international organizations and 178 national societies.

Scope of Work: More than 115 million Red Cross volunteers work worldwide.

An Organization Is Born

In the 1800s, battles were fought very differently than they are today. Soldiers rushed at one another on foot or on horseback. Those killed instantly were often much luckier than those who were wounded. Injured soldiers were often trampled or left to die from their wounds.

Medical treatment was limited and very basic. Medical workers trying to retrieve wounded soldiers from the battlefield were often attacked. If these workers succeeded in reaching the injured, they had little to offer them. There were no painkillers to ease their pain.

Compassionate people of the 1800s did not know how to help. They were afraid of being attacked if they did lend a hand. When disaster struck, they lacked organization, protection, and supplies.

Businessperson Henry Dunant was appalled by the suffering of wounded soldiers. He made it his goal to organize, protect, and equip civilians to ease the suffering caused by battle.

Dunant formed a committee and organized an international conference in Geneva, Switzerland, in 1863. The committee proposed that in times of peace, volunteers should be trained and supplies stockpiled for use in times of war. The committee also stated that these volunteers would be considered neutral in times of war and would be recognized by the sign of a red cross.

In 1864, the committee's recommendations were accepted at another international conference in Geneva. The Red Cross movement had begun.

> "Although modern weapons have changed today's warfare, they generate the same results as 100 years ago: prisoners of war and civilians in need of protection and basic assistance."
>
> **Caroline Moorehead, Red Cross and Red Crescent Magazine**

Quick Fact •

Henry Dunant was nicknamed "The Man in White" because of the white suit he wore when he helped the injured soldiers at the battle of Solferino.

PROFILE

Henry Dunant

Henry Dunant arrived in the Italian town of Solferino on June 24, 1859, near the end of a huge battle. He looked in horror as men were cut down and left to die. He saw soldiers mercilessly killing wounded men. He felt the killing was butchery and **inhumane**. The mass suffering he witnessed as the sun rose the next morning was even worse.

At daybreak, he walked amongst more than 40,000 dead, dying, or injured soldiers. Many men begged to die. Their suffering was unimaginable. Dunant plunged in to help. He also organized the few local villagers, mainly women and children, that he could find.

Many villagers did not want to help their enemies. Dunant convinced them by saying *tutti fratelli*, which means "all brothers." The villagers responded and cared for the wounded regardless of their nationality.

> "Would it not be possible, in times of peace, to form relief societies for the purpose of having care given to the wounded in wartime?"
>
> **Henry Dunant, from** *A Memory of Solferino*

Although the civilians were untrained and lacked supplies, Dunant organized them to help. They followed Dunant's orders, changing bandages and giving water to the wounded.

In 1862, Dunant wrote and published *A Memory of Solferino*. In it, he outlined a plan to improve the care of wounded soldiers. This book would become the basis of both the Red Cross and the Geneva Convention.

While Dunant's work with the Red Cross brought him fame, it did not bring him fortune. Dunant was often forced to live off the charity of others.

In 1901, Dunant was awarded the Nobel Peace Prize. He died nine years later at the age of 82.

The Mission

In order to relieve human suffering, the Red Cross and Red Crescent Movement follows seven basic principles:

> " ... to humanize war is not to encourage it, but to spread a spirit of peace in the midst of war which can contribute towards its conclusion."
>
> **Yves Sandoz, ICRC**

Humanity

The Red Cross is set up to lessen the suffering of people worldwide. Its purpose is to protect life and health. It promotes understanding and peace among all the people of the world.

Impartiality

The Red Cross is impartial. This means it does not treat anyone differently because of nationality, sex, race, religion, or political views. It helps people based on their need.

Neutrality

The Red Cross does not take sides in wars of any kind. Red Cross workers help victims on both sides of a battle.

Independence

The Red Cross is independent. The national societies cannot be forced by their host countries to act against the Red Cross's humanitarian ideals.

Voluntary Service

The Red Cross is set up to help people and not to gain anything by doing so.

Unity

There can only be one Red Cross or Red Crescent society per country.

Universality

The Red Cross is a worldwide organization. National societies work together to help people all over the world.

In 2001, the Red Cross distributed more than 140,000 tons of relief supplies, such as food and clothing.

The mission of the International Red Cross and Red Crescent Movement is:

- to prevent and alleviate human suffering wherever it may be found

- to protect life and health, and ensure respect for the human being, in particular in times of armed conflict and other emergencies

- to work for the prevention of disease and for the promotion of health and social welfare

- to encourage voluntary service and a constant readiness

Source: *The Seville Agreement, 1997*

Key Issues

Health

Poor health and medical need are among the most obvious signs of suffering. As a result, health care has been a focus of the Red Cross and Red Crescent Movement since its beginning.

In addition to providing medical support in times of conflict, the Red Cross also provides health programs in peacetime. One of the most important peacetime health programs is blood and tissue donation and distribution. The Red Cross also provides vaccines for diseases, such as measles, to people who cannot afford them.

" With the high cost of prescriptions today, many ... are forced to choose between food and medication. The most rewarding benefit for me is seeing the relief that comes when we are able to get them the medications they need."
Sarah Wick, American Red Cross

During the war in the former Yugoslavia, the American Red Cross established feeding programs for more than 60,000 people in central Bosnia.

Education

The Red Cross considers health education to be an important way to prevent suffering. The Red Cross offers first aid courses, water safety courses, and **HIV/AIDS** education. Red Cross workers go into communities and schools to teach adults and children how to stay safe while working, playing, and living. They also teach people about diseases and how to avoid getting them. The Red Cross believes that by providing people with opportunities to learn, the suffering in the world will decrease.

CASE STUDY
First Aid Education in Action

In October 2000, Charles Mitchell took the Red Cross First Aid and **CPR** courses as part of his training to become an instructor at the YMCA. His training was soon put to the test. On April 5, 2001, Mitchell was working at Lee Hunter Elementary School when he witnessed a student choking. "I saw this little girl with tears in her eyes and her face was a dark color blue," said Mitchell.

The student was 11-year-old Jessica Williams. "I started choking and I started to see dark dots.

> "When you go through the emotions of saving someone's life, it's something that never leaves you."
> Charles Mitchell

I just thought I was going to die because I never choked that bad before in my life."

Using his training, Mitchell first confirmed that Jessica was actually choking. "I asked her if she was choking just to see if she could respond. She couldn't say anything."

Once Mitchell knew that Jessica was choking, he moved behind her to perform abdominal thrusts. It took two quick thrusts and the piece of food was dislodged.

For Mitchell, the experience was unforgettable. "She kept saying, 'Thank you sir, I just knew I was going to die.'"

It has made me realize how precious life is ... I don't know what I would have done if I didn't have the emergency lifesaving training from the Red Cross."

Blood and Tissue Donation

Millions of people require blood every day. The Red Cross is a leader in collecting and distributing life-saving blood and tissue. Of the more than 75 million **units of blood** that are collected worldwide each year, Red Cross and Red Crescent societies are directly responsible for 30 percent. Another 30 percent is donated by organizations that are supported by the Red Cross.

The American Red Cross collects more than 6 million units of blood a year. However, in the United States alone, 25,000 more people need to donate blood each day to keep an adequate supply for future disasters.

Blood Safety

While blood donations can save lives, contaminated blood can be dangerous. It is important that donated blood be free of alcohol, drugs, viruses, and parasites. While donated blood goes through a testing system, one of the best ways to ensure safe blood is at the source—the donor. Healthy donors give healthy blood.

It has been proven that blood coming from volunteers is less likely to be contaminated than the blood from paid donors. As a result, the Red Cross now only supports voluntary blood donor clinics.

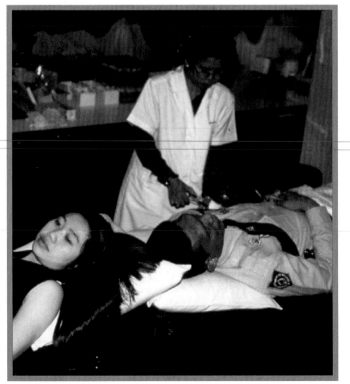

A blood donor must be between the ages of 16 and 60, weigh at least 100 pounds, be in good health, and not have taken medication in the three days prior to giving blood.

CASE STUDY
Bone Donor a Hero

David Ruggia is a normal 12-year-old child who loves to run and play. One day, David fell off a horse and was unable to get up. Doctors found that he had no upper end to his femur. A big cyst had left this part of his bone hollow. Doctors said that David would never walk again.

David's father, Bud, refused to give up and took his son to a special surgeon. The surgeon said that David was "shattered like humpty dumpty," but that they would try to put him back together again.

"Thanks to the gift of a bone donor, crushed bone was packed into the cavity. We waited again as, week after week, David's body grew fresh bone through the **matrix** provided by the donor. Each x-ray showed the bone becoming denser and denser, until Dr. Wilkens was finally satisfied. It was time for yet another surgery—David's third."

After painful physical therapy and hard work, David was able to walk, run, and play again. Bone donation has allowed David to resume his favorite activities.

"How I wish I could hug the bone donor who made the miracle possible!" said Bud. "If the bone operation had not succeeded, David would never have walked again."

Since it began in 1982, the American Red Cross Tissue Services has helped more than 600,000 people get back on their feet.

Poverty

Poverty is another source of suffering. People who are poor may not have enough money to pay for food, shelter, or medical care. When people cannot afford the necessities of life, they suffer physically and mentally.

In developing countries, many people cannot afford or do not have access to food and water. The Red Cross brings safe drinking water and emergency food to communities in need. It also teaches these communities new methods of growing food so that people can not only eat, but can also sell food to make a living.

Poverty is found on the street corners of almost every city in the world. The Red Cross provides job training for homeless people so that they can earn money and afford shelter and food. The Red Cross also has trained volunteers who bring medical aid to those who cannot afford it.

Discrimination

Many people are treated unfairly because of their race, sex, political ideas, sexual orientation, or religion. This is discrimination, and it causes widespread suffering in the world. The Red Cross does not **discriminate**. It helps people based on need.

Every year, Red Cross and Red Crescent societies assist more than 200 million people worldwide.

CASE STUDY

Red Cross Workers: Breaking the Silence

In the battle against AIDS, one of the Red Cross's biggest challenges is getting people to talk about it. In many countries, there is a prejudice against individuals with HIV/AIDS. Many people refuse to help infected victims or even to learn about the disease. This silence increases the suffering of those with HIV/AIDS as well as their families, friends, and communities.

Some companies discriminate against people with HIV/AIDS. They may fire employees discovered to be infected. These companies do not understand how HIV/AIDS is spread or how the employees may have caught the disease. The Red Cross is taking a stand against HIV/AIDS discrimination—starting with its own organization.

There are currently 200,000 Red Cross workers with HIV/AIDS. While many other businesses and organizations try to hide infected members, the Red Cross sees infected volunteers as a resource. Infected people have firsthand knowledge of the disease, and they can teach others what they know.

HIV-positive Red Cross workers are teaching the people in their communities what HIV/AIDS is and what it means for not only those who have it, but also for their families, their employers, and for the community at large. Prevention is also a focus of these teachings. The Red Cross believes that getting people in the world to talk and learn is the first step in reducing the suffering caused by HIV/AIDS.

Around the World

The International Red Cross and Red Crescent Movement is truly an international organization. Since the movement began in the late 1800s, national societies have been founded in nearly every country in the world. Today, there are 178 national Red Cross societies.

Countries with national Red Cross or Red Crescent societies are colored in yellow. Countries that are in the process of forming a society are labeled and colored red.

TUVALU

COOK ISLANDS

N

MICRONESIA

KAZAKHSTAN
ISRAEL
PALESTINIAN RED CRESCENT
ERITREA
COMOROS

U.S. Operations

Humanitarian Clara Barton founded the American Red Cross in 1881. Since then, the organization has experienced impressive growth, fueled by the compassion of the American people.

Today, more than 1 million volunteers work for the American Red Cross. They help with approximately 70,000 national disasters a year. The American Red Cross not only helps people within the United States, it is also a part of international relief efforts.

The American Red Cross offers many services to those in need. Some of these services include:

• The Armed Forces Emergency Services helps keep military personnel abroad in touch with their families.

> **"Volunteers are the very foundation of the American Red Cross ... One in every fifty-six Americans is a Red Cross volunteer or volunteer blood donor."**
>
> Gregory L. Smith, American Red Cross

• Biomedical Services provides plasma donation and ground-breaking medical research.
• Community Services provides job search assistance for the homeless and brings hot meals to seniors at their homes.
• Health and Safety Services instructs lifeguarding and babysitter training courses.
• International Services organizes food programs.
• Disaster Services trains people to respond to natural disasters.
• Nursing Services provides direct medical assistance in times of need.

The Red Cross immediately responded to the September 11th terrorist attacks by providing food, shelter, and health care for those in need.

CASE STUDY
Clara Barton: Founder of the American Red Cross

"I may be compelled to face danger, but never fear it, and while our soldiers can stand and fight, I can stand and feed and nurse them."
Clara Barton

Clara Barton was born on Christmas Day in 1821 in a small town in Massachusetts. Clara became a teacher and founded several schools in New Jersey. During the American Civil War, Clara became a volunteer. She was known for her compassionate nature. Even though women were not allowed on the battlefield, Clara often forced her way onto the field so that she could cook and care for the troops. She became known as the "Angel of the Battlefield."

After the war, Clara traveled to Europe and learned of the Red Cross. After working alongside members and witnessing their work, she returned to the United States determined to set up a national society. Clara believed that the United States could benefit greatly from a humanitarian organization such as the Red Cross.

Clara worked hard for five years to convince politicians that the United States should create a national Red Cross society. In 1881, she succeeded, and the American Red Cross was born.

Clara served as president of the American Red Cross from 1881–1904. During that time, she led disaster relief efforts for victims of forest fires, floods, droughts, famine, tornadoes, hurricanes, tidal waves, and yellow fever outbreaks in the United States and abroad. She also led relief efforts for military and civilian victims of the Spanish–American War. Clara Barton brought organized humanity to the United States under the flag of the Red Cross.

Milestones

The Red Cross and Red Crescent Movement has been helping victims of tragedy for more than 140 years. Since its founding in the 1860s, the Red Cross has grown into an international organization that is known throughout the world.

1884: The Little Six

Six children put on a play that raises $50. The children donate the money to the American Red Cross. This is the first known youth activity of the American Red Cross. The money aids a family victimized by a severe flood in the Midwest.

"Sometime again when you want money to help you in your good work," the children wrote to Clara Barton, "call on the Little Six."

1828

Henry Dunant is born in Geneva, Switzerland.

1859

Henry Dunant, witnessing the bloody aftermath of the Battle of Solferino, bandages, feeds, and comforts the sick and dying. He encourages other civilians to help.

1862

Dunant's book, *A Memory of Solferino*, is published. In it, Dunant proposes that permanent relief societies should be trained to help casualties of war.

1863

The Committee of Five is formed in Geneva, Switzerland, to put Dunant's idea into practice.

1864: The First Geneva Convention

Diplomats from sixteen countries meet at a conference in Geneva, Switzerland. At this conference, The Geneva Convention for the Amelioration of the Condition of the Wounded in Armies in the Field is signed. This convention binds the signing countries to protect and humanely treat sick and wounded soldiers and the people caring for them. The symbol of the Red Cross is adopted as a protective emblem.

1867

The First International Conference of the Red Cross is held to discuss humanitarian issues.

1870

The Red Cross records the names of prisoners of war so that their families know they are alive.

1876

The Committee of Five adopts the name International Committee of the Red Cross.

1876

The Turkish government adopts a red crescent on a white background, instead of a red cross, to represent relief workers. Other Islamic countries soon do the same.

1881

Clara Barton forms the American Association of the Red Cross and lobbies the government of the United States to sign the Geneva Convention.

1914–1918: World War I

During World War I, demands on the Red Cross increase. In addition to caring for wounded soldiers, the relief workers visit prisoner-of-war camps and call for improved conditions for the prisoners. They send parcels to prisoners and give information on captured military personnel to their families. The Red Cross protests against the inhumane treatment to which both combatants and civilians are subjected during the war. The Red Cross leads a campaign against the use of chemical weapons, which made their first mass appearance during the war.

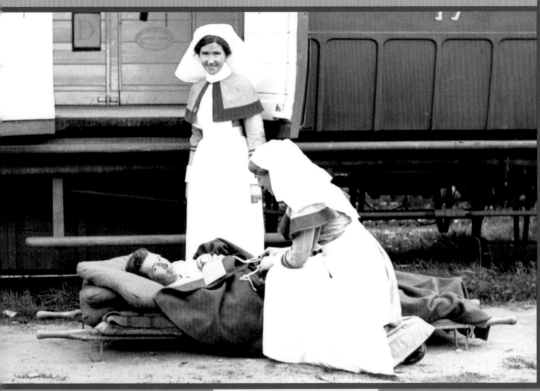

1910

Dunant dies at the age of 82.

1914

At the start of World War I, the International Red Cross sets up the International Prisoners-of-War Agency. It has the task of collecting and passing on information on captured servicemen and forwarding relief parcels to them.

1917

The International Committee of the Red Cross wins the Nobel Peace Prize.

1917

The American Junior Red Cross is formed.

1919

The League of Red Cross Societies is formed as an association of Red Cross societies worldwide.

1929

The first and second Geneva Conventions are updated. A third convention is adopted, protecting prisoners of war. The Red Crescent emblem is officially recognized.

1882

The United States signs the Geneva Convention, allowing it to become part of the International Red Cross.

1899

At the Hague Convention, rules respecting laws and customs of war are agreed upon. The protections granted at the 1864 Geneva Convention are adapted to include victims of sea warfare.

1901

Dunant is awarded the Nobel Peace Prize.

1906

The first Geneva Convention is revised and expanded.

1907

The 1899 Hague Convention is expanded, and the principles of the 1906 Geneva Convention are adapted to maritime warfare.

1943

U.S. President Franklin Roosevelt, the honorary chairperson of the Red Cross, declares the month of March "Red Cross Month."

1944

The International Committee of the Red Cross wins the Nobel Peace Prize.

1948

May 8, the birthday of Henry Dunant, is declared World Red Cross and Red Crescent Day.

1949

The first three Geneva Conventions are updated. A fourth convention is added. The new addition allows for the protection of civilians detained in enemy countries or occupied territories.

1960

The Central Tracing Agency is formed from the Prisoner-of-War Agency. It locates prisoners of war and keeps them in touch with their families.

1960–1970

There is a rapid increase in the number of national societies in the Red Cross and Red Crescent Movement.

1939–1945: World War II

During World War II, the Red Cross works to help prisoners of war and wounded soldiers. It organizes food parcels for war victims. While the Geneva Conventions cover the rights of prisoners of war, civilians, such as those held in concentration camps, are not covered. As a result, the Red Cross is unable to help them. This leads the Red Cross to revise the Geneva Conventions to include civilians detained in enemy or occupied territories. During the war, Red Cross workers travel more than 6 million miles, the equivalent of 400 trips around the world.

1985: Aid for Africa

The Red Cross launches a massive African relief campaign to help feed millions of starving people. Providing food, seed, transportation, communications, nursing, medicines, and administration of the relief effort are some of the ways that the Red Cross responds. In all, the international Red Cross agencies distribute almost $250 million in aid to more than 2.25 million people—mostly mothers, pregnant women, the elderly, and small children in twenty-one African countries.

This increase follows the newfound independence of many former colonies in Africa and Asia.

1963

The League of Red Cross Societies initiates a large development program to aid countries in Africa and in the Caribbean that have gained independence.

1963

The International Committee of the Red Cross and the League of Red Cross Societies jointly win the Nobel Peace Prize.

1965

The Seven Fundamental Principles of the Red Cross—humanity, impartiality, neutrality, independence, voluntary service, unity, and universality— are announced.

1960-1980: Vietnam

The Red Cross helps soldiers, civilians, and refugees during the Vietnam conflict. After the Vietnam conflict, many Vietnamese orphans are brought to the United States and adoptions are arranged for them. Teams of American Red Cross nurses, other volunteers, and paid staff work around the clock to greet the exhausted infants and children, and provide them with nursing care.

1996: Aid for Former Yugoslavia

The Red Cross and Red Crescent Movement provides food, water, and medical assistance to about 900,000 civilians in the former Yugoslavia, as a result of hardship caused by the conflict in Bosnia-Herzegovina. Red Cross workers visit detainees being held by hostile forces and help families separated by the conflict to re-establish contact with their loved ones.

1990–1991

The Red Cross and Red Crescent Movement aids prisoners of war, civilians, and refugees in the Gulf War.

1991

The League of the Red Cross and Red Crescent Societies becomes the International Federation of Red Cross and Red Crescent Societies.

1974

The American Red Cross begins teaching people how to save lives with CPR.

1977

Additional **protocols** are added to the Geneva Conventions. Protection is extended to victims of armed international conflicts and to victims of armed non-international conflicts.

1983

The League of Red Cross Societies changes its name to the League of Red Cross and Red Crescent Societies.

1986

The International Committee of the Red Cross, the League of Red Cross and Red Crescent Societies, and the national Red Cross societies become known as the International Red Cross and Red Crescent Movement.

2000

After shootings of students at Columbine High School in Colorado, in 1999, and similar incidents elsewhere, the American Red Cross creates a Safe Schools Task Force to develop and put into place a nationwide program to address youth violence in American communities.

Current Initiatives

HIV/AIDS

HIV/AIDS is one of the most dangerous diseases humans have ever faced. HIV is a virus that infects humans and causes them to get sick much easier than they normally would. Once someone with HIV becomes sick, their illness is called AIDS. HIV/AIDS touches on many of the goals of the Red Cross. It is an issue that relates to health, education, poverty, and discrimination.

> "Emergencies happen every year, especially in the Caribbean. But HIV/AIDS is here every day. Every minute of the day."
>
> **Mark Scott, Jamaican Red Cross**

AIDS is destroying lives worldwide at an alarming rate. There are currently more than 36 million people living with HIV/AIDS. In Zimbabwe, one in four people between the ages of 15 and 49 are infected with the virus. Those living with the disease need medical help and above all, knowledge and support.

The Red Cross wants to help those with HIV/AIDS, and prevent others from getting the disease.

People suffering from the physical effects of HIV/AIDS are not the Red Cross's only concern. In some countries, so many people are now infected that there are not enough people to fill jobs. This leads to poorer countries and millions of orphans.

The Red Cross intends to reduce HIV/AIDS-induced suffering by:

- establishing voluntary testing in communities
- creating counseling services and self-help groups
- teaching HIV/AIDS prevention in schools and communities
- providing in-home medical care
- encouraging governments to work harder at controlling the disease
- working to get medication to those who cannot afford it

Quick Fact •

In the southeast African country of Zambia, 1,200 teachers are trained each year, but 1,500 teachers die in that same time from AIDS-related illnesses.

CASE STUDY
AIDS in Kenya

Mary was only 25 years old when her husband died of AIDS. Before his death, he had refused to be tested for AIDS. He even refused to discuss the disease. When Mary had herself tested, she discovered that she, too, was HIV positive.

In Mary's village, it is customary for a widow to remarry. Mary did not want to remarry. She knew that any future husband she might have would also catch the disease.

Mary's relatives did not approve of her decision. They stopped supporting her and her three children. They accused her of using HIV as an excuse not to remarry.

"They want me to go along with tradition," she says, "but I know that if a man inherits me he'll get the disease, and I've decided I don't want to give it to another person."

The Kenyan Red Cross supports Mary's decision not to remarry. They give her advice on health care, as well as help her plan for the future. Once a week, Mary takes a trip to the local Red Cross office. At the office, she can discuss her problems in private.

Through the Red Cross, Mary has been introduced to a self-help group for people living with HIV/AIDS. The Red Cross hopes that such projects will encourage more people to speak out about AIDS. It is only then that Red Cross workers can teach them to help themselves and learn to live positively.

"I am very worried about my children. How will they live in the future if I'm not here? If I die they'll be left alone and I know nobody will take care of them."
Mary

Cord Blood Donation

The Red Cross is also a leader in medical research and innovation. One new idea is umbilical cord donation. The umbilical cord is the passageway between mother and child for nutrients and oxygen during pregnancy. The umbilical cord is often thrown away after a baby is born. Red Cross researchers are now working to change this.

Each year, 30,000 children and adults are diagnosed with leukemia, genetic immune disorders, and other blood diseases. The blood remaining in the umbilical cord after birth could be very valuable to these people. It contains stem cells, which are cells that allow the human body to produce all other blood cells. If these people are able to get a cord blood transplant, there is a good chance that their lives may be saved.

The new stem cells travel to the bone marrow spaces, where they begin to multiply. Over time, the stem cells in the transplanted cord blood replace the patient's diseased or damaged bone marrow and immune system. Cord blood donation is a very positive step for people with blood diseases and cancer.

Cord blood stem cells can be given to patients after cancer treatments, such as chemotherapy or radiation, have destroyed their own stem cells.

For donors, the process is easy. The collection process takes less than three minutes. Instead of throwing out the umbilical cord after a baby is born, a doctor or midwife collects the blood that remains in the umbilical cord. The small amount of blood remaining in the umbilical cord, about 5 ounces, is drained and taken to the American Red Cross cord blood bank to be frozen. The American Red Cross is now assembling the first nationwide Cord Blood Bank Program.

CASE STUDY
The Power of Humanity

In May, 1999, the slogan "The Power of Humanity" was chosen to represent the Red Cross and Red Crescent vision worldwide until 2004. This slogan is meant to inspire and assure people. It is intended to remind people that everyone has the ability and responsibility to help those who suffer.

The Red Cross defines the power of humanity as:

- *Our capacity to bring out the best in people and to nurture their latent willingness to work together to help others, making this willingness a powerful force, not a latent one. The willingness of Red Cross and Red Crescent volunteers and staff to commit time and energy to create solutions and deliver services—this is the power of humanity.*

- *Our capacity to be an organized channel for those who recognize that when there is so much talk about human rights, there is also the need to accept a certain responsibility. Touching people with our ideas and persuading them that they too wish to make a commitment—this is the power of humanity.*

- *Our capacity to be a willing partner. Cooperating with organizations and people who share a common concern for those most in need, and who recognize the need to work together to achieve common solutions—this is the power of humanity.*

Source: *The International Federation of Red Cross and Red Crescent Societies*

"Our mission remains to improve the lives of vulnerable people. We can achieve this mission only through mobilizing our national societies and volunteers—the power of humanity."
Dr. Astrid Heiberg,
President International Federation of Red Cross and Red Crescent Societies, 1999

Take Action!

Become an active and responsible citizen by taking action in your community. Participating in local projects can have far-reaching results. You do not have to go overseas to get involved. You can do service projects like the ones the Red Cross volunteers do no matter where you live. In fact, young people are helping out every day. Some help support overseas projects. Others volunteer for service projects in their home communities. Here are some suggestions:

Donations are important to the Red Cross. Many people choose to donate their time. Young people up to age 24 make up 40 percent of all Red Cross volunteers. By donating your time to the local Red Cross, you will be helping people in need. You will also learn life-saving skills, which can last a lifetime.

Each local chapter of the Red Cross has different needs. In Zimbabwe, the Red Cross Society youth clean garbage off streets, fetch firewood for elderly villagers, and help people repair their huts. In the United States, your local Red Cross may need your assistance packaging food parcels. Your time can help meet many different needs.

If you want to help, look up your local Red Cross on the Internet or in the phone book. Give them a call to see what help they need.

The American Red Cross has created an on-line community of caring kids called the CyberSquad. To become a member of the CyberSquad, you can volunteer at the local Red Cross, take a course in first aid, donate blood, volunteer at a local blood drive, or donate $15 to the Red Cross. To learn more about the CyberSquad, write an e-mail to: cybersquad@usa.redcross.org

Where to Write

International	United States	Canada
International Federation of Red Cross and Red Crescent Societies PO Box 372 CH-1211 Geneva 19 Switzerland	**ICRC in the United States** 2100 Pennsylvania Ave. NW, Suite 545 Washington, DC 20037	**Canadian Red Cross National Office** 170 Metcalfe St. Ottawa, ON K2P 2P2
International Committee of the Red Cross 19 avenue de la Paix CH 1202 Geneva Switzerland	**American Red Cross in Greater New York** 150 Amsterdam Ave. New York, NY 10023	**Red Cross in Quebec** 6, place du Commerce Ile-des-Soeurs Verdun, QC H3E 1P4

In the Classroom

EXERCISE ONE:

Make Your Own Brochure

Organizations such as the Red Cross use brochures to inform the public about their activities. To make your own Red Cross brochure, you will need:

- paper
- ruler
- pencil
- color pens or markers

1. Using your ruler as a guide, fold a piece of paper into three equal parts. Your brochure should now have a cover page, a back page, and inside pages.
2. Using your color markers, design a cover page for your brochure. Make sure you include a title.
3. Divide the inside pages into sections. Use the following questions as a guide.
   - What is the organization?
   - How did it get started?
   - Who started it?
   - Who does it help?
4. Using the information found in this book, summarize in point form the key ideas for each topic. Add photographs or illustrations.
5. On the back page write down the address and contact information for the local Red Cross office.
6. Photocopy your brochure and give copies to your friends, family, and classmates.

EXERCISE TWO:

Send a Letter to Your Congressperson

To express concern about a particular issue, you can write a letter to your member of congress. This can be an effective way to make the government aware of issues that need its attention. To write a letter, all you need is a pen and paper or a computer.

1. Find out the name and address of your congressperson by contacting your local librarian. You can also search the Internet.
2. Write your name, address, and phone number at the top of the letter.
3. When addressing your letter, use the congressperson's official title.
4. Outline your concerns in the body of the letter. Share any personal experiences you may have that relate to your concerns. Use information found in this book to strengthen your argument.
5. Request a reply to your letter. This ensures that your letter has been read.
6. Ask your friends and family to write their own letters.

Further Reading

American Red Cross Staff. *American Red Cross Babysitter's Handbook*. St. Louis: Mosby Inc., 1998.

Espeland, Pamela, and Barbara A. Lewis. *The Kid's Guide to Service Projects: Over 500 Service Ideas for Young People Who Want to Make a Difference*. Minneapolis: Free Spirit Publishing, 1995.

Handal, Kathleen. *The American Red Cross First Aid and Safety Handbook*. New York: Little Brown & Co., 1992.

Whitelaw, Nancy. *Clara Barton: Civil War Nurse*. Springfield, NJ: Enslow Publishers, Inc., 1997.

Web Sites

IFRC Youth Page
www.ifrc.org/youth
The International Federation of Red Cross and Red Crescent Societies Youth Page is an ideal starting point for young volunteers who are interested in working for the Red Cross. There is a youth directory as well as links to youth activities around the world.

Virtual Blood Donation
www.redcross.org/services/youth/izone/tours.html
This "Virtual Blood Drive" offers a step-by-step explanation of the donation process. It was created by a Red Cross youth volunteer. The site requires a Flash player.

American Red Cross Museum: Activities for Youth
www.redcross.org/museum/actkids.html
The American Red Cross Museum has created an activity page for children. The site includes stories and a reading list of interesting books on the Red Cross.

Glossary

AIDS: a disease that slowly destroys the body's natural ability to fight off other diseases; stands for acquired immune deficiency syndrome

CPR: an emergency procedure used on someone whose heart has stopped; stands for cardiopulmonary resuscitation

discriminate: treat people differently because of race, religion, sex, or political ideals

femur: leg bone that attaches to the hip

HIV: a virus that destroys the body's capacity for immunity; stands for human immunovirus

humanitarian: a person or organization devoted to the well-being of humans

inhumane: lacking in compassion or kindness

matrix: fiber structure inside bone tissue

protocols: new rules added to a treaty

units of blood: a unit of blood is about 15 ounces; the average human has 10 to 12 units of blood in his or her body

Index